I0490282

50 THINGS TO KNOW ABOUT THE CULTURE OF CUTE

EXPLORING CUTENESS

Lauren C. Johnstone

Cover designed by: Ivana Stamenkovic
Cover Image: https://pixabay.com/photos/pets-cute-cat-dog-cute-wallpaper-3715733/

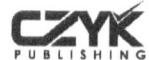

CZYK Publishing Since 2011.

50 Things to Know

Lock Haven, PA
ISBN: 9781673561524

50 THINGS TO KNOW ABOUT THE CULTURE OF CUTE

BOOK DESCRIPTION

Do cute things melt your heart? Would you love to know the reason why we find some things cute and others not-so-cute? Have you ever wondered why most cute things seem to originate in the Far East? If you answered yes to any of these questions then this book, Exploring Cuteness, is for you.

50 Things to Know About Cuteness by Author Lauren Candice Johnstone offers a glimpse into a world where rainbows, emojis, unicorns, cartoons, and childish good-looks abound and thrive. Most books on the subject offer in-depth explanations backed by scientific and marketing jargon. Although there's nothing wrong with that, I am simply offering a light-hearted glimpse into this phenomena and, by no means, claim to know it all.

Based on knowledge extracted from articles and studies by leading experts, as well as blogs and corporate information, I have pieced together a compilation of 50 facts that you may, or may not, know about the phenomenon of cuteness.

In these pages you'll discover what makes people or things cute, the darker side of cute, cute tech, and many little fun tidbits of information. This book will help you open your mind to various perceptions of attractiveness, particularly in the differences between Eastern and Western ideals of beauty and femininity. The book is divided up into sections for easy navigation.

By the time you finish this book, you will know so much more about a topic you may never known had so many facets to it, so grab YOUR copy today. You'll be glad you did.

TABLE OF CONTENTS

DEDICATION

This book is dedicated to my son, Bjorn Joon Johnstone, who is the light of my life. I would also like to dedicate this book to all of my furry friends who brought me so much joy over the years.

Lauren C. Johnstone

ABOUT THE AUTHOR

"The individual has always had
to struggle to keep from being
overwhelmed by the tribe. If you try
it, you will be lonely often, and
sometimes frightened. But no price
is too high to pay for the privilege
of owning yourself."

— Friedrich Nietzsche

Lauren Johnstone is a graduate of the University of Cape Town. She graduated with a Bachelor of Arts degree in Media & Writing, Film and Visual Studies, and English Literature in 2004. She was placed on the Dean's Merit List twice, both in 2002 and 2004, and received an invitation to become a member of the Golden Key International Honour Society in 2003, which she accepted.

Lauren spent 2.5 years teaching English as a Foreign Language to middle school and high school kids in South Korea between 2008 and 2011 and completed her TEFL certification during this period.

While in Asia, she came into contact with many aspects of South Korean culture and the cuteness she encountered there left a lasting impression, especially when contrasted with the noticeable lack of it in her home country, South Africa.

Currently, she currently works remotely as a Transcriber, Virtual English Trainer, and Freelance Writer. Lauren Johnstone has provided her services independently and through online employment forums. She is a member of the South African Writers' Circle, which she joined in 2018 in order to develop her writing skills. She has a love of foreign languages, most notably Spanish, Italian and Turkish. She also picked up some basic Korean whilst abroad and can read Hangul, the Korean alphabet.

Lauren loves animals. Rabbits, hamsters, guinea pigs, a black Labrador named Max, a ginger cat named Percy, and a baby tortoise named Billy are amongst the many pets she's owned since childhood. Music is one of her many passions. She started playing classical acoustic guitar when she was just 8 years old. In 1999 she received the Trinity College London Music Exam Certificate for successfully completing the grade 8 classical guitar exam. Before entering university, she completed a one-year Diploma in Audio Engineering at Cape Audio College and briefly worked as an Assistant Sound Engineer backstage at a popular theatre called Artscape.

If you would like to get ahold of Lauren Johnstone, you can get in contact with her through Twitter: https://twitter.com/Laur3nCJohns

Introduction

"... cuteness is an addictive antidote to today's pressured expectations of knowing our purpose, being in charge, and appearing predictable, transparent, and sincere."

Simon May, The Power of Cute

I guess you're wondering why anyone would want to write a book about cuteness, right? I know it does seem like a bit of a frivolous topic, not serious enough to have a whole book dedicated to it. Well, the truth is that I've had a penchant for wide-eyed puppy dog stares, adorable infantile trinkets and statuettes, furry, fluffy animals, and everything in-between. Actually, it's somewhat of a "thing" for me.

I think part of the appeal for me is that it's simply light-hearted and fun. Cute things are indicative of innocence too. I mean, babies are cute, right? And maybe I just want to hold onto that aspect of my being, before the seriousness of adulting put a kink in my carefree world. The funny thing is, as non-serious and shallow a topic as being just plain darling may seem, when you dig deeper you find that it's a very complex topic with many layers to it, so there is plenty to be discovered.

With this book, I aim to unveil some of these layers of cuteness, as we know it, by exploring everything from cartoon characters, psychology and marketing to physical appearance, animal cruelty and cute home appliances.

Who knew cute could be so complicated? I certainly didn't, not until I decided to write this book! I hope that you learn as much as I did during this writing process and have fun reading it.

LOOKS

1. BABIES PROVIDED US WITH OUR CUTE BLUEPRINT

"Babies should be classified as an antidepressant. It's pretty hard

to be in a bad mood around a 5-month-old baby."

Jim Gaffigan, Stand-Up Comedian

Baby schema is a theory that says that cute physical features basically just make you want to reach out and care for babies. Even animals and objects have these features. Who came up with this idea? None other than Austrian native and zoologist Konrad Zacharias Lorenz. You can't talk about cuteness without this man's popping up.

2. WHEREVER YOU ARE IN THE WORLD, CUTE IS CUTE

No matter where you are in the world, you'll find that the people around you respond to the same cute features. Really, it's just hard-wired into us it seems. The really fortunate side to this is that it ensures we don't go around dumping our babies and pets onto others. Or worse, abandoning or neglecting them altogether. Cuteness is a necessity that ensures parents care for their kids, so that we can continue populating this wonderful giant blue-green ball we call Earth.

That being said, I have to say that the Far East takes the cute factor to another level. I love shopping in South Korea because of the sheer volume and variety of colorful cartoon characters plastered all over products that you wouldn't even think to associate with cuteness. Stationery shops are a favorite haunt of cutie pies such as Hello Kitty and friends.

3. NEWBORNS ARE NOT THE CUTEST OF THEM ALL

You no longer have to feel a pang of guilt the next time you look at a newborn and think, "Woof, she's ugly." I'm not being mean. A study carried out by a team of researchers at Brock University have confirmed it, newborns aren't that cute. Just ask Tony Volk, an Associate Professor in Child and Youth Studies at the University in St. Catherines, Ontario, who carried out this study along with Prarthama Franklin and Irisa Wong.

They got straight to the point by naming the study, "Are newborns' faces less appealing?" The study asked 142 adults to rate the cuteness of 18 babies from newborn to 6 months old. Interestingly, it was found that babies around 6 months old were most likely to be adopted. These results are not that surprising once you understand the evolutionary reason behind it.

In the past, newborns were the least likely to survive because of illness or food shortages, so it was practical to make sure your older kids were sorted out first, rather than the newborn, who was least likely to survive. We've actually evolved to stop ourselves from becoming too attached to them. If this seems cruel, Professor Volk explains that this is just a coping strategy to lessen the grief they'd feel if the newborn dies. Basically, it's survival of the fitness at play, whether we realize it or not.

4. EVEN 3-YEAR-OLDS RECOGNIZE CUTENESS WHEN THEY SEE IT

Adults are in the habit of comparing cute babies but so are kids! Researchers at the University of Lincoln were curious to find out when humans start to notice *baby schema*, those set of features that make one appear cute in the eyes of others. In their quest, they carried out two experiments. The participants? Kids aged 3 to 6-years-old.

In both experiments, a group of children was asked to look at 2 sets of pictures. One set contained pictures of adult humans, cats, and dogs, the second set contained pictures of baby humans, cats, and dogs. These pictures were digitally manipulated to include baby schema. Then, they were altered again to look less cute. The first time the kids were asked a simple question along the lines of which pictures they found cute. The second time no questions were asked, but their eye movements were tracked to see which pictures really captured their attention. Sneaky as it may seem, it's a good way to figure out which images were most attractive to their kiddie brains.

Findings revealed that kids preferred the cuter versions of each set of images, meaning that baby humans won over adult humans and baby animals won over adult humans. If there were a Grand Supreme award for the overall winner, baby animals would win, even over baby humans. This research was published in the journal called *Frontiers in Psychology*, which pretty much makes it official.

5. FEMALE REPRODUCTIVE HORMONES PLAY A CRUCIAL ROLE IN WHAT WE SEE AS CUTE

Just as you may have suspected, men and women perceive cuteness in different ways. Women turned out to be more reliable at selecting the cuter infants in a study done by Researcher and Lecturer, Janek S. Lobmaier, from the University of Bern in Switzerland.

Furthermore, women who were younger or hadn't gone into menopause yet were even better at this. There is a clear link between female fertility, female reproduction, maternal instincts and cute babies, which makes sense. Really, it's just biological. Females who are ripe for fertilization tend to be more empathetic towards young ones as they are potential mothers in the making.

6. MAKE YOURSELF CUTER BY WEARING CIRCLE LENSES

Circle lenses are all the rage in the East. These are bigger than regular colored contact lenses and therefore give the impression that your iris is bigger than it is. The point is to give you a doe-eyed appearance, bringing you one step closer to looking like a dolly. And if that's not good enough, it also ages you in reverse. Yep, circle lenses are a cheaper alternative to the fountain of youth.

7. WHEN YOU'RE CUTE IT'S HARD TO BE SEXY

"I'm not trying to be sexy. It's just my way of expressing myself when I move around."

Elvis Presley

Try as you might to show people flames your sizzle just isn't hot enough when it's extinguished by your cuteness. That "freakum" dress makes you look like an imposter and the response you get stays the same, "Awww.... Look how cute you look!"

Guys may pass you over because while you are cute enough to warrant a look, you're not hot enough to make their eyes jump out of their heads. Hot girls just have an edge and guys are... well, guys!

The real peeve is when you're legitimately angry about something and your anger gets met with a smile because you look even cuter when you're angry! With babyish features softening your scowl, it's hard to be taken seriously, but let's face it, better to be cute than neither cute nor hot! Count your blessings.

FEELINGS

8. JUST LOOKING AT A CUTE PICTURE STIRS FUZZY FEELINGS IN US

Apparently, when we look at pictures of things we identify as cute, the brain waves in our orbital frontal cortex (which I will refer to as OFC from hereon) start going crazy, sending messages to the brain. Professor Stephan Hamann, at Emory University in Atlanta, Georgia, checked it out. He confirmed that the part of the brain that responds to fear and arousal shows increased activity when observing things we find endearing. Now I know why I think, "Aw…" for no reason every time I look at bug-eyed animals unless it's a Colossal squid because… Just, no.

9. SOME PEOPLE ARE SADDENED BY CUTENESS

"Cute is defenseless, needy, non-threatening and therefore ripe for abuse."
"... cute masks cruelty with a bow."

Jenny Morber, Freelance Science Journalist

Well, this is quite a morbid way to look at something that usually inspires smiles in most people, but I think what she means is that because of the state of the world we live in today, the violence, bullying, inconsideration, selfishness, and just plain nastiness, then yes, an adorable mite will surely suffer. How could cuteness be a mask for cruelty you ask? Apparently, some of those cutesy YouTube videos you circulate to friends and family were created through non-animal friendly means.

10. CUTENESS AND EMPATHY ARE LINKED

*Cuteness has been
conceptualized as a moral emotion
leading to empathy or compassion
as part of a moral circle*

Sherman & Haidt, 2011

We've established that cuteness evokes maternal instincts and nurturing behavior in adults, especially adult women of child-bearing age. Empathy is necessary in order to lovingly take care of another human being. If you abandoned your baby it would be frowned upon by society. In fact, anyone who falls short of being a "good" mother, as defined by society, is in danger of being visited by social services. Why? Well because taking good care of your baby is the right thing to do. So, it turns out that baby schema is necessary and you, as a mother or father, have a moral obligation to fulfill.

11. SEEING CUTE CREATURES OR SNIFFING BABIES MAKES YOU WANT TO CHOMP THEM

Not for real though, it's just play-biting. A few nibbles here and there can satisfy your cute cravings. Also, in a weird and seemingly twisted way, it creates bonds of trust. Like, "Look at you. You're so cute I wanna eat you! I'm nibbling your cheeks and I could bite you at any moment, but I won't 'cos you can trust me!"

12. DID YOU KNOW THAT CUTENESS CAN TRIGGER AGGRESSION?

There's a term for it; it's called cute aggression. How did these two opposites come together? Well, my understanding is that the process goes something like this. Girl sees a cute puppy, brainwaves go crazy in the OFC, too many brain waves = cuteness overload, brain tosses in some aggression to balance you out before you go off your cute rocker, and voilà, cute aggression is born.

Now, instead of squashing the puppy to death you simply squeeze it lovingly without suffocating it. Cute aggression saved the puppy! I would equate cute aggression with an overdose of cuteness, or overload. Yes, it happens and, yes, there's a cure.

13. THERE'S A FINE LINE BETWEEN CUTE AND CREEPY

"Let's flip a coin. Heads, I'm yours. Tails, you're mine."

Unknown

Now I'm not talking about animals or cartoons here. I mean, when people try to be cute but end up on the opposite end of the spectrum entering Freakville. Let me paint a picture for you. You managed to find an acceptable cute guy among the Tinder hopefuls and exchange flirty texts. Before long he's sending tons of heart emojis, lovestruck faces and just going overboard with the cute thing in general.

Well, unless you're a narcissist who thinks that that's the kind of behavior you obviously inspire in people, it's likely to be a huge turn off because it's just too much. You can barely tell if it's desperation or craziness after a while and from then onward it's just a downward spiral ending in deletion. Nobody wants that kind of weirdness in their life.

14. "AW" SEEMS TO BE THE UNIVERSAL RESPONSE TO CUTENESS

"Origin: Natural exclamation: first recorded in American English in the mid 19th century."

Lexico Dictionary at lexico.com

Certains sounds are associated with certain emotional reactions. However, cuteness is not an emotion that is recognized. When you're feeling cute, what exactly would you call that emotion? Compare this to fear, which has been studied to death, and has many terms associated with it to describe this emotion.

Professor Buckley, from Griffith University, says that there is barely any research in the field of what is sometimes called cute-emotion. There is no word for the emotion associated with feelings of cuteness even though there are many words to describe it.

You may have noticed that I've spelled aw with one "w". Some people spell it with two, which is technically incorrect but acceptable. Some people draw out their "aw" to "awwwww…." as if the more w's you add the cuter the object of this cute-emotion. Aw, not to be confused with awe, is defined as an exclamation in the Oxford dictionary meaning that it is a response.

Although psychology recognizes cute-emotion as a thing, is still remains nameless and we are stuck with our "oohs" and "aws" when responding to cuteness. According to Professor Buckley, this is a surprising language deficiency and the main reason given for this namelessness is that only modern societies have had to deal with and respond to cuteness. Really, it boils down to the fact that despite the biological functions cuteness has served since forever, the social function is still new and a characteristic of modern societies.

15. CUTE-EMOTION IS EXPLOITED

"Advertising is legalized lying."

- H. G. Wells, English Writer

Advertisers often appeal to our soft spot to get us to buy products and/or services. What mom can resist a TV advertisement showing a cute toddler begging his mom to buy the latest sandwich spread? Imagine you're sitting on your sofa watching the idiot box with your child, an advertisement flashes across the screen complete in technicolor and goofy characters asking you to purchase something your toddler would absolutely love. You look over to your left (or right) and your kid looks back at you with puppy dog eyes. Now, you're cornered by both ad and child while your motherly urge to make your child happy tugs at your conscience. Do you see where I'm going with this? In reality, we make purchasing decisions with our hearts when we should be using our heads.

16. WE ARE LESS LIKELY TO EAT THE MEAT OF AN ANIMAL WE LABEL "CUTE"

"... when animals are cute enough, they might become too sweet to eat."

Janis H. Zickfeld

A sociologist named Liz Grauerholz did a study showing that we are able to eat meat by distancing ourselves from the animals that we are consuming in our minds. We distance ourselves through the language we use, through the packaging, and marketing/advertising.

Advertisements do this in two ways. One is to show the meat in a way that is so far removed from the actual animal it came from, that we have to make a big leap in our heads to imagine the animal it came from. The second way is to show the animal as super cute, so cute in fact that it no longer seems real, and we can go on and eat our steaks in peace because in our heads that cute animal isn't really the subject of cruelty.

We distance ourselves from what's really happening because as long as it's not real we don't have to deal with all our conflicting emotions. This dissociation is known as the "meat paradox". We want to see ourselves as moral, good human beings, and not as savages who are eating the meat of animals that are being farmed and abused in the process. How can you be for animal rights and still consume meat?

A study by *Ruby and Heine* (as cited in Zickfield, et al, 2017) shows that people are less likely to eat the meat of ugly or cute animals. This is because we feel disgusted by the ugly animal and empathy for the cute one.

17. DOGS BRED TO BE SMALLER AND CUTER SUFFER

*"No matter how you're feeling,
a little dog gonna love you."*

– Waka Flocka Flame, American Rapper

Socialite Paris Hilton popularized the designer dog, or teacup puppy, which is a tiny cute ball of fluff you spoil, dress up and carry around in a designer bag. Popular micro dog breeds are Chihuahuas, Yorkshire Terriers, Shih Tzus, Pomeranians, Pugs, Poodles, including Maltese Poodles, and Silky Terriers.

What you may not know, is that some of these dogs are purposefully bred to be even smaller in size, which results in many painful defects such as weak bones, pain, digestive problems, and breathing difficulties. In fact, they often collapse from overheating and just the pure struggle for air. Pups are sometimes starved to prevent their growth. The mothers also have difficulty giving birth. Despite all these negative aspects, the demand for these tiny dogs is so great that breeders let their standards slide in order to make a quick buck. Nevermind that their tiny bladders can barely hold their pee and little urinal presents will greet you in every corner of your home, but they are high maintenance and need to be fed several times a day due to their tiny tummies, which can't hold a regular-size doggy meal.

The miniature breed fad is not exclusive to dogs The Scottish fold cat has a rather cute genetic mutation that gives them tiny floppy ears, long whiskers. On the flip side, this same mutation results in arthritis, making movement difficult and painful, as well as changes in the jaw size, which affects how they eat.

No matter how much you yearn for a teacup puppy or strangely cute owl-looking cat, remember the long list of health issues, the pain these creatures endure and their unavoidable shortened life spans before seeking them out.

18. VIDEOS OF CUTE ENDANGERED ANIMALS CREATE A DEMAND FOR THEM

"If you can't sleep, count sheep.
Don't count endangered animals.
You will run out."

Mitch Hedburg, American Comedian

This surprising fact is based on a 2016 study of a video that went viral on Twitter showing a ring-tailed lemur receiving back rubs from some Madagascan kids. When they stopped the lemur would demand more. People thought it was adorable and I bet you would too, so they shared the video on Twitter and Facebook. Unfortunately, all this posting and sharing created a demand for pet lemurs.

But how did researchers find this out? Well, by analyzing a whopping 14,000 tweets plus Google and YouTube searches. They found huge spikes in phrases relating to finding and having a pet lemur shortly after the video was posted. Now that's some serious SEO! Of course, there was no evidence of any such purchase or exchange actually taking place, but it was a worrying trend. An opportunistic wildlife trafficker could take advantage of such a sudden high demand for wildlife creatures and cash in while the hype is rife.

Apart from traffickers pulling lemurs from the wild left, right, and center, another serious concern is the way that people are perceiving wildlife, i.e. cute and cuddly pets. You might need to rethink that selfie with the cute chimp the next time you're out and about vacationing. Your wildlife selfies might give the impression that these animals are, in fact, not really endangered and that they're tame enough to take home to join your old pal, Fluffy, back at home.

19. YOU MAY WANT TO RETHINK CUTENESS WHEN IT COMES TO CERTAIN ANIMALS

Yes, it's true, looks are deceiving. Nowhere is this more apparent than in the animal kingdom. I mean, how could a cuddly koala bear or an itty-bitty hamster have a dark side? Well, actually koalas carry STDs, hamsters are little alcoholics, penguins kidnap baby penguins and wombats will chew your face off. Quite a few animals murder their young for various reasons, animals such as the polar bear, lions, hedgehogs, and hamsters. Yes, that popular pet for kids is really a little monster. There's a list of animals that engage in horrendous behavior that we'd much rather stay in the dark about, but it's good to know what you're dealing with when coming face-to-face with one of these "cutie pies".

20. UGLY ANIMALS NEED TO BE PRESERVED TOO

"It's funny how the ugly duckling always has so many beautiful things to teach us."

— Curtis Tyrone Jones, Author

There are a number of groups around who raise awareness about endangered animals. The popular and well-known World Wide Fund for Nature, or WWF, is one of them. They have an easily recognizable panda as a logo, a cute creature we would all like to save, I'm sure. But there are other less visually appealing animals that need rescuing too. The problem is that they don't qualify in the beauty stakes, so they receive much less attention.

That's why the Ugly Animal Preservation Society was formed in 2012, to raise awareness around endangered animals who are not that cute, but who need saving too. I know that name that so bluntly points out the animals' bad looks doesn't foster the right feelings and may make you feel sorry for those animals. Founder, Simon Watt, uses his background in biology, TV presentation and stand-up comedy to highlight these animals' predicament. There are workshops, funny videos and shows to watch that are both informative and entertaining.

21. PUPPIES ARE CUTEST AT 6 TO 8 WEEKS OLD

Just like human babies have a window of peak cuteness, puppies also have such a window. According to a study carried out by researchers from Arizona State, Utrecht University and Texas Tech

University, 2 to 3 months old is when puppies are at their peak cuteness.

A bunch of college students, 51 to be exact, were asked to rate which puppies, out of a choice of three breeds, they found most attractive. The sample of puppies offered was newborn to 7 months old. The two to three month age range won. Interestingly, this is around the same age that puppies are often abandoned by their mothers.

Apparently, most of the dogs in the world are strays and abandoned puppies are commonplace. Discarded by their nonchalant moms, with no way to defend themselves, they have to switch on the charm to snag a new owner who will care for it, fend for itself and hope for the best, or face The Grim Reaper. I'm sorry to say this, but it really is a dog eat dog world.

22. THE QUOKKA WAS NAMED THE WORLD'S HAPPIEST ANIMAL

This small nocturnal herbivore is an endangered species with a selfie-worthy smile. Quokkas are Australia's cutest animals and always have a huge smile plastered across their faces, which makes great selfies but is actually a method of keeping themselves cool in the hot climate. They are cat-sized marsupials who live mainly on Rottnest Island, a tiny island near Perth.

23. PENGUINS DO A PEBBLE 'PROPOSAL'

Sea otters hold hands while sleeping, penguins propose with pebbles, seahorses flirt and whales sing to attract a mate. I have to say that the penguin proposal really stood out to me because these flightless birds are super cute already, but the pebble proposal story really strummed my heartstrings. Penguins live in the coldest regions of the world, making their way among ice and polar caps, scary polar bears and icy winds. A little bit of cuddle weather is great and penguins know all about keeping warm using body heat, as they huddle together. I guess, for them, it's huddle weather!

Male penguins select the smoothest pebbles he can find and offers it to his lady love. She shows her acceptance of him by placing his pebble in her nest. Also, there is such a thing as monogamy among birds, as some breeds of penguins mate with the same partner every year. Heartwarming indeed.

CORPORATE CUTENESS

24. EMOJIS MAY NOT BE APPRECIATED BY YOUR BOSS

They're cute and relay a message, or feeling, fast and effectively. Emojis have become the hieroglyphics of the modern world. However, they're short of the professionalism you need to maintain at work, so please don't use them when texting your boss why you're late for the second time that week. Keep it between yourself and your buddies.

25. EMOJIS COULD ALSO LAND YOU IN HOT WATER

We all know that Facebook is a minefield of privacy issues, as is Google and other online platforms. These internet-related products and services can bombard you with advertisements, so you need to be mindful when being cutesy from your work devices. They can track your devices, which again, your boss is not going to appreciate. Also, your emoji-glyphics can be misunderstood and then used against you resulting in potential lawsuits! Despite the fact that it could be bad timing on your part, do you really want to take that gamble?

26. CUTESY LOGOS CAN UNDERMINE YOUR COMPANY

If your company has zilch to do with babies, animals, kids, and the like, then it might be a good idea to think twice before opting for an adorable logo if you want to be taken seriously in your chosen industry. Since cuteness is associated with youth,

35

playfulness, and fun, it is also associated with frivolousness and inexperience and that is not the message you want to send potential clients. I know it's a bummer but try to keep the cute contained when it comes to your money.

27. BEING CUTE WILL GET YOU EVERYWHERE

If you're seeing green because you suspect your cute co-worker got that promotion you wanted because of their cute factor, you might just be right. There is evidence to prove this. A study called the "lost letter technique" sent out resumes with pictures of fictional males and females, some cute and some not-so-cute, in the States and Kenya. The cute people's resumes were posted more often. Yes, looks do matter

On the other hand, the race of the jobseeker also seemed to play a role because African American males had no luck, while white men had some.

THE FAR EAST

28. A BUNCH OF JAPANESE TEENAGERS STARTED JAPAN'S KAWAII CULTURE

If it weren't for a bunch of wayward Japanese girls we'd be robbed of the joy of kawaii. The word kawaii itself is said to be over 1,000 years old, but its meaning has changed over time. Tired of the strictness of their society, some creative teens decided to doodle their way out of the bonds they felt were stifling them.

While the rest wrote their characters vertically, as they should, the "naughty" girls wrote theirs horizontally, changed letter shapes and inserted their own girly doodles. They were basically saying, "No! We will not write the way you want us to write. We will create our own writing that is way cuter!" You'd be forgiven for thinking a child dawdled all over their books, but that's the idea, a cute rebellion if you will. Sure, it makes sense, and it's the subtlest rebellion I've ever heard of.

29. KAWAII SPILLS OVER INTO EVERY ASPECT OF JAPANESE LIFE, INCLUDING FASHION

Apart from kawaii being a form of escapism for teens seeking a breather from the oppressive expectations of everyone around them, it was also a way to get men to like you more and want to marry you. And what better way than to make yourself look like a helpless damsel in need of rescuing and protection? Enter kawaii fashion; it does a great job of drawing attention to young women.

There are plenty of Japanese fashion styles to mimic: Lolita, Decora, Angura kei, Kuroi Niji, Gyaru, Ganguro, Kogal, Bōsōzoku, Visual kei, Oshare kei, Cult party kei, Dolly kei, Fairy jei, Mori kei and Kimono style. I know that first name caught your attention. You're thinking, "Lolita?" I know the first thing I think of when hearing that word is the 1997 movie by the same name starring Jeremy Irons. That was a pretty hectic flick, to say the least. I mean, a preteen coupled with a man, old enough to be her grandpa? Yet, that is exactly the look these rebellious Japanese teens were going for.

Lolita fashion is exactly as the name implies, dressing like a much younger girl and looking all cutesy. Think bows, frills, pigtails, and basically looking like a little doll. Throw in a bit of gothic influence and you're good to go.

30. HELLO KITTY IS THE MOST FAMOUS KAWAII CHARACTER

"Not every girl is a Hello Kitty girl. But those who are... are just happier"

Hello Kitty

Do you remember when Hello Kitty was trending? She was everywhere! Her simple face was plastered all over stationery, mugs, clothing, jewelry and more. She never really went away though, did she? And by the way, her real name is Kitty White. Yeah, she lives near London, not Japan or China, which seems a bit odd. She's an international star, so I guess she can live wherever she wants. After all, she is only the second richest animated character in the world and the richest kitty in the world having earned $80 billion to date! A lady called Yuko Shimizu brought her to life in 1974.

If you think Hello Kitty is cute, you should meet her friends. There are so many, about 400 of them! You should meet My Melody, Keroppi, Gudetama, and Piochacoo. They're pretty awesome, just like she is, although not quite on the A-list that Kitty White has found herself on.

31. CUTE IN THE EAST IS DONE DIFFERENTLY THAN IN THE WEST

If you need proof, take a look at Instagram. All you have to do is compare selfies from Far Eastern countries like Korea, Japan, and China with selfies from places like the United States, UK, Australia, and Europe and you will see a definite difference. Let me break it down for you. In the West, women love the following: tanned skin, a sexy pout, contoured make-up, thick and defined eyebrows, skimpy and/or figure-hugging clothing. In the East, women love this:

super pale skin, huge eyes, a small mouth, an oval face, innocent facial expressions, cute photo effects like rabbit ears, bows, and so forth.

One reason given for this difference is that being cute is safer than being sexy. That makes sense in places with strict societal norms. Being too sexy in the East will get you nothing but "bad looks".

32. IF YOU WANT TO EXPERIENCE DIGESTIBLE CUTENESS, JAPAN IS THE PLACE TO GO

Over 1,000 years ago, traces of cuteness were already appearing in Japanese cuisine as is pointed out by Sei Shonagon in The Pillow Book, which refers to a child's face being painted on a melon. There are other examples where food is made to be a visual treat, such as the elite samurai's ritual of eating "honzen ryori", a way of carefully arranging dishes and served on legged trays.

Fast forward to the present and Japanese moms are lovingly arranging and packing their kids' school lunches or bento boxes, as they are known in the Land of the Rising Sun. The cute twist on the traditional bento box is kawaii bento, where food is made to resemble popular cute cartoon characters. The rectangular- or square-shaped box is packed tightly with similarly shaped bite-sized foods such as rice/noodles, some type of meat, deep-fried food, sushi vegetables, salads, omelets, and so forth, making the food easy to transport and easy to consume. Nowadays bento boxes can also be purchased, saving time and effort.

Also known as, kyaraben or charaben, which is short for Character Bento, these lunches are popular amongst adults and kids who follow the trend of visually consuming your food. From the honzen ryori enjoyed by the samurais to kaiseki meals adorned with a season-changing ornament, such as a flower or leaf, to taffy-makers molding sugar syrup into animal shapes to post-WWII, when kawaii made its way into food culture.

Crafting a kawaii bento box can literally take hours, but this doesn't stop Japanese moms from creating these daily works of lunchbox art for their loved ones. If you ever open your lunchbox to see a hot dog with legs and eyes, remember to tell your mom that you love her.

OBJECTS

33. OBJECTS ARE CAPABLE OF CUTENESS TOO

Take a walk through any toy store and you will see toys that have human characteristics. Apart from literally painting eyes and a smiley mouth on a toy car, they can be cute just by being small. Also, we think about childhood when we set eyes on them. The biggest culprits are definitely plush toys. Their size matters, as tiny usually equals cute but bigger objects can be cute as well. This particular trait of consumer products is called whimsical cuteness and it's a big moneymaker.

In his article "Behavioral Bias Bingo — The Whimsical Cuteness Effect," Ross Steinman summarizes research published in the *Journal of Consumer Research* by Nenkov and Scott in 2014. To summarize, it was found that while looking at cute babies and animals led to more thrifty and careful behavior, looking at whimsically cute objects led to more spending. Part of the reason is that consumers viewed the objects as fun and playful.

34. *BE MY MOTHER* IS A RANGE OF CUTE HOME APPLIANCES THAT MIMIC BABY BEHAVIOURS

Be My Mother is a Japanese range of cute home appliances created by Hyerim Shin. The cute factor is to encourage owners to care for their products, to make chores more fun and to bring happiness. The range consists of a toaster, vacuum cleaner, and trash bin. Hyerim Shin's rules of cuteness were used in the design of her products. These are threefold: baby schema behavior, baby schema shape, and baby schema color. Just like a baby, her products require attention and maintenance. By applying these rules, she has created a product that is cute in appearance and behaviours thereby encouraging affection for the product.

Three key baby behaviors were chosen for each appliance to imitate. These are sneezing, pooping and playing peekaboo. Sneezing was best-suited for the toaster, which sneezes leftover crumbs. Pooping was appropriate for the vacuum cleaner, which wiggles and "poops" out the dust bag once its full. Lastly, the trash bin lets you know it's time to take out the trash by playing hide and seek.

35. CUTE SOCIAL ROBOTS CHANGE HOW HUMANS AND MACHINES INTERACT

At the end of 2017, a bunch of social, domestic robots were getting ready to enter our homes as members of our family. For this to happen as seamlessly as possible, we need to trust our robot friends. We also need to care for them and be close to them as if they were human. Their cuteness makes us drop our guards and forget that they are machines, networked to other smart devices, capable of storing valuable and private data about yourself and your family. They're there looking cute and being super helpful, assisting you with running your household and being a non-judgmental friend.

Picture yourself welcoming your new robot friend into the family in all it's cute, helpful and impressive glory and watch as it takes direction while remaining harmless. Also, it has many cool features, one of which is to interact with its human user. They're living with you inside your home, but they are a piece of machinery, a type of computer that is being fed intimate details about yourself and your loved ones that you may not even be aware of.

Just like computers can be hacked, so can a robot. Your seemingly harmless and vulnerable robot friend has collected some very valuable data, data that can be used against you or to influence you. Who really has the power in this scenario? You or the robot?

36. THE 90S BEANIE BABIES CRAZE RESULTED IN TRAMPLED CHILDREN AND MURDER

"At a market in Connecticut, fanatical collectors trampled children to get their hands on the retired tie-dye "Garcia" bear."

Zachary Crockett, 19 May 2018

These cute plush toys, filled with plastic pellets (or beans) that made them more flexible, were the brainchild of the eccentric Ty Warner. Warner cashed in big-time during the Beanie Babies craze and became a billionaire in the process. Thanks to their plastic filling, these toys could be bent to do things like sit or wave, for example. Some of the first babies to see the light of day were Legs the Frog, Pinchers the Lobster, Splash the Whale and Patti the Platypus, to name a few. Initially, these darlings cost only $5 and were very affordable for most people, but they were only available at certain stores.

Warner made sure that his employees were close-mouthed about information related to the toys so that consumers never knew how many of a certain 'baby' was available or where it would be sold. When certain babies all but disappeared from store shelves, it created a craze in people who literally went hunting for those missing babies. When these babies were "found", they sold for much more than their actual value, which was only $5. Some sold for thousands of dollars online.

The thing about Beanie Babies is that they become an investment for many people who bought them with the intention of then selling them at a later stage when they were worth more money. A lucky few cashed in on the craze, but tons of people lost not only their hard-earned money but friends and partners too. An old man stole thousands of Beanie Babies and, another man shot a security guard over a Beanie Baby dispute while smuggling rings were in full swing at the border. Finally, 1999 was the year that marked the end of the Beanie Babies craze and thank goodness for that. These adorable toys really brought out the worst in people.

37. BARBIE WAS ORIGINALLY A BACHELOR PARTY GAG GIFT

"If Barbie is so popular, why do you have to buy her friends?"

Steven Wright

Let's face it, Barbie is the western ideal of beauty, and as such she never really took off in the East. Supposedly, the German Bild Lilli doll from the 50s was the inspiration behind Barbie who rose to fame in the 60s thanks to the Handler family and her association with the Mickey Mouse Club.

The sexy and suggestive Lilli, who was and based off of an adult comic strip, caused quite a stir amongst concerned mommies who thought her svelte figure was not child-friendly. The Handlers, on the other hand, wanted Barbie to be a vessel that little girls used to forge their way into the world. She represented a world full of choices. Basically, the message is that Barbie's done it all and so can you.

38. HELLO BARBIE RECORDS YOUR CHILD'S PRIVATE CONVERSATIONS TO MAKE MONEY

Gone are the days where you had to use hand puppets and make them talk, eyes threatening to fall off while you hide behind your mom's tattered couch making squeaky voices to entertain yourself and your friends. Today we have voice recognition technology, which can bring children's beloved toys to life. If you'd been hoping to avoid your child giving you the side-eye for even suggesting a puppet show, you may have stumbled upon Hello Barbie. She's glam, she talks and she has a huge vocabulary for a doll.

I was curious as to what kind of conversation Barbie might be interested in, so I had a look at Mattel's 261-page long pdf located on Mattels' website. Here there are lists of everything she's currently able to utter. Conversation topics range from friendship to school to fashion to animals to dreams and so on. Some lines are really nice and seem quite motivational.

For example: "I bet someone who's a friend to animals knows a thing or two about being a friend to people." Or, "You know, on those days where waking up for school is hard, I just think about how much fun it'll be to see my friends." Then, there are some bordering on eerie, like "(LAUGHING) Sorry, I was just trying to remember this song… (HUMMING AGAIN) hmm, hmm, hmm…" Finally, Hello Barbie asks some repetitive personal questions such as, "So you have two sisters? So you have three sisters? So you have four sisters?" I thought, "Wow, she's really digging for info."

And this is why moms are up in arms. Just like any electronic device, Hello Barbie faces privacy issues and data breaches. Could you really sleep soundly knowing your precious pumpkin is happily chatting up a storm with what amounts to a recording machine in the next room, giving away her secrets and/or family information, easily gotten by big corporations that store that data for their own commercial use? No, I didn't think so. Her white T-shirt may say, "Hello, Hello, Hello," but I think most savvy parents would rather say, "Bye, Bye, Bye."

39. MICKEY MOUSE HAS HAD MANY MAKEOVERS

*"I only hope that we never lose
sight of one thing – that it was all
started by a mouse."*

Walt Disney

All you need to see are those iconic set of ears to know Mickey Mouse is in the house. Corny, I know, but whatever. Disney's Mickey Mouse was born in 1928 at Walt Disney Studios. He looked quite different back then. Basically, he lacked color, was shoeless, gloveless, and less cute facially. Thank goodness an animator called Fred Moore gave him a makeover back in 1935.

Mickey's had so many makeovers I can't help but think he'll have more work done in the future. He's even had a nose job! Honest, his nose is shorter now, cute as a button. Clearly, the mouse has no sense of fashion, or could it be a sense of time because he's been wearing the same clothes since forever despite the fact that it's been almost a century since those have been drawn on him! Those oversized red shorts, huge yellow shoes, and those white gloves that are so big I sincerely wonder how he gets anything done. But it really doesn't matter in the end because everybody loves Mickey. Do you need proof? Well, he has own star on the Hollywood Walk of Fame. Quite an achievement for such a tiny fella. Well done, Mickey.

PSYCHOLOGY

40. YOU CAN STRENGTHEN YOUR MARRIAGE WITH CUTE THERAPY

"Marriage is like a walk in the park... Jurassic Park."

- Unknown

What's the first thing you think about when you think of your spouse? Does the thought cause you to feel more loving or less loving towards him or her? Couples who no longer have that loving feeling start thinking about leaving and some try therapy before making the break. Traditional therapy involves many pricey appointments, lots of talking and a great deal of ongoing hard work to keep the spark alive.

Psychologists at Florida State University did a study to see if there was a different, less expensive, and easier way to change how we think about our spouse and they found it. Humans have a habit of unconsciously making connections between things that exist together, no matter how random and it's called automatic associations.

The study involved showing couples a series of pictures of cute things like puppies, or banal objects, or positive words, and then flashing a picture of their spouse in-between those every so often. After a few weeks, couples noted an improvement in how they perceived their spouse. Their brains had been tricked into making new positive associations with their spouse!

41. YOUR PET CAN HELP LIFT YOUR MOOD

"When you feel lousy, puppy therapy is indicated."

- Sara Paretsky, Author.

There's a reason why we associate spinsters with lots of cats, and there's nothing bad in that. The elderly are often neglected by a youth-obsessed society, and while all their friends are starting to push up daisies, why shouldn't they seek comfort in a furry friend?

Animals are able to provide things that humans cannot. They're much more tuned in to your emotions and therefore there is a sense of a special intimate bond between pet and owner. They're always there for you, so they're reliable. They're pleasing to look at, or you wouldn't have chosen that particular pet to adopt or purchase. They snuggle you when you need it and taking care of them makes you feel useful in a world where you may feel useless.

Their furry mugs get you out of bed in the morning to feed them. They keep you on a schedule. Dogs get you out of the house for their daily walk, even when you want to hide from the world. The wonderful end result is you get some fresh air and maybe even make a few new friends along the way with other pet owners doing the same thing. That will definitely chip away at feelings of isolation.

For those who struggle physically, cats are easier because they basically take care of themselves, no walks needed, playtime optional. If you're seriously strapped for cash, a smaller critter will still do. Think hamsters. If you really don't have the time, cash or energy but still need a boost, you can pet-sit or just spend time around other people's pets. Heck, I'm sure your neighbor will be grateful if you offer to walk their mutt every now and again without seeking a cash reward!

42. ANIMALS CAN PLAY THE ROLE OF THERAPIST FOR YOU

"The best therapist has fur and four legs."

Unknown

We've established that dogs, cats, and hamsters can help get you out of a depression, but did you know that animals help people suffering from Post-Traumatic Stress Disorder (aka PTSD), autism, and many other mental illnesses too? Some animals are trained, while others just provide emotional support. Either way, they are a great crutch for us humans to lean on in times of stress and need. Miniature horses, chinchillas, and other animals are all great choices for a human in need of emotional support. They help reduce your need for medication, which your kidneys will thank you for because they are sparing your body the extra work it needs to do digesting pills and potions.

Animals use their amazing intuitive abilities to sense oncoming anxiety attacks and calm their humans down. They help autistic individuals to socialize. The only problem with relying on your pet is that certain public spaces are not as welcoming of them, and may not permit them to enter the premises.

Dogs can even help someone suffering from schizophrenia! When you're losing touch with reality, all you need to do is check your dog's cute face, check his reactions to his environment and make sense of things from there.

43. THE TEDDY BEAR EFFECT

"A room without a teddy bear is like a face without a smile."

- Gill Davies, Author

No, it has nothing to do with the popular stuffed toy. The Teddy Bear Effect is a term coined by Kennedy School lecturer, Robert Livingston. He did research into the correlation between earning potential, facial features and race. He found that high-earning black CEOs are baby faced and, as a result, are viewed as non-threatening. This is in contrast to the stereotypical black male, who is seen as aggressive and hypermasculine, even dangerous. Their paler counterparts, white male CEOs, had no such luck, nor did women. In fact, female CEOs would want to avoid looking baby-faced because society is programmed to view females as non-threatening already. Therefore, a female CEO would be more concerned with appearing competent than cute.

44. WE HAVE DIFFERENT EXPECTATIONS OF CUTE KIDS

"If You Want Your Children To Be Intelligent, Read Them Fairy Tales. If You Want Them To Be More Intelligent, Read Them More Fairy Tales."

Albert Einstein

The curiosity of kids is sometimes overshadowed by their cuteness. Paintings and drawings that reveal a child's inquiring mind are often overlooked and brushed off as cute, rather than viewed seriously. What if the child has their own ideas about the world around them? What if the way he or she drew something was a "commentary" about the world they live in rather than just a cute work of art for arts' sake?

Beth Sebesfi, an early childhood educator and mother of three, challenges adults to see the world from a child's perspective. She proposes that kids are more insightful and thoughtful than we may realize and that we can actually learn something from them. Basically, she argues that children are held to low expectations, which is possibly too low, which then has a negative impact on how we interact with them and how we understand them. In doing so, we are robbing both ourselves and the kid from learning more about one another and that educators are missing an important chance to be even better educators.

45. YOU MIGHT THINK OLD PEOPLE ARE CUTE BUT DON'T BABY-TALK THEM

"Old people's speech is not to be dishonored -- after all, they saw the sun first."

African Proverbs

You know how you slow down your speech and talk a little louder and chop your sentences up, so that your aging gramps can hear and understand you?

Yeah, don't do that, unless they're suffering from dementia or something similar. Yes, you thought you were being helpful, but as it turns out, your "gramps" may be fuming underneath his soft wrinkly exterior you find so darn cute.

This change in speech patterns when communicating with the elderly is called "elderspeak" and it's a bit of a problem. If you're unfamiliar with it, all you have to do is pop down to your nearest nursing home and you'll get an earful, as it is most commonly heard in this kind of environment. For some reason, we tend to baby the elderly, perhaps because we see them regress mentally and physically and feel sorry for them. We think we're being helpful by slowing down and shortening our speech while singing our words, inserting a few pet names here and there for good measure and asking and answering questions for them.

Well, it's really not good for the elderly as it makes them feel inferior, incapable, confused and stupid. We see 'cute' videos of old people doing regular things that have been re-labeled as cute because they are on the wrong side of 50. Remember, old people are not children, they are adults who do adult things.

LANGUAGE

46. IN 1730 CUTE HAD A TOTALLY DIFFERENT MEANING

If you had called someone cute in 1730, you were actually telling them how smart and observant they were, but really it was a quick way of saying acute, minus the "a". A century later its meaning did a 360 and it took on its current meaning. Funnily enough, we still find traces of its 1730s meaning in phrases like, "Don't get cute with me."

47. THE URBAN DICTIONARY DESCRIBES A "CUTE ATTACK"

Similar to an overdose of cuteness, you can suffer from a "cute attack." Episodes occur when the amount of cuteness in front of you causes an involuntary response in your body that feels as if you are 'under attack.' You experience physical symptoms, such as chills up your spine, smiles, giggles, squeals, and involuntary nervous ticks. You just can't help yourself and the end result is that you are a helpless victim overcome by cuteness.

ART

48. CREATE YOUR OWN CUTE CREATURES WITH AMIGURUMI

Amigurumi is a Japanese technique of creating plush toys by knitting or crocheting. The usual goal when making amigurumi is creating something kawaii. No matter whether you're new to the craft or have been knitting away for years, it's possible for anyone to do. All you need is yarn, a small gauge crochet hook, stuffing, pipe cleaners if you want to make your creation bendable and little pebbles to weigh it down so that it can stand. You can make characters, scenery, household objects or mini food items. Cute amigurumi dolls appeared in Japan in the 70s, but it really boomed in popularity in the 2000s once it reached US soil.

49. A JAPANESE ARTIST MAKES SWEETLY SINISTER ART

A Japanese painter called Yoshitomo Nara straddles the line separating sweet and sinister. He paints, sculpts, makes prints, ceramics, and installations. His preferred subjects are cute animals and children, but his version of cute has an eerie aura. The themes he explores through his art are definitely not cute, but serious issues that face society, such as isolation, an important theme in today's technology-filled world where more and more people are suffering from loneliness. He also explores rebellion and spirituality. The artist claims that his work is confused with the popular manga and because of this people fail to see the serious themes being explored in his art, which is far from the case.

A quick Google search on Nara's work conjures up quite a number of cute-looking girls, exhibiting all the baby schema necessary to make you go, "Aw." Yet, these girls all have a menacing look on their faces, they're cute, but they're scary too. You want to go, "Eek," instead. His work shows that cute can be twisted and that cute and scary can uncomfortably exist together, and that is definitely not cute.

50. AN ART EXHIBITION TAKES CUTENESS DOWN A PATH TO REGRET

The Kristen Lorello Art Gallery held an art exhibition that took cuteness down a sickeningly sweet path to yearning and regret. During the period 10 July to 14 August 2019, the New York art gallery exhibited the works of contemporary artist, Scott Alario, called "*Can You Dream It? (Yes I can.)*," which uses the theme of cuteness in a disruptive way. You're transported back to a time where playtime was boundless and loops back to this time in a nostalgic way that is cyclical and filled with regret.

Leftover materials commonly used by kids for arts and craft projects, such as paintbrushes, glitter, ribbons, Play-Doh, and the like, are used and combined in new ways that create a kind of tension between the happy realm of childhood where dreams were big and the future was bright, and the present realm of the viewer, where childhood dreams are possibly unfulfilled and there is a sense of regret. Confronting the cuteness of your childhood may not be all that peachy keen after all.

OTHER HELPFUL RESOURCES

If you're still itching to know more about cuteness, the following links will help satisfy your curiosity:

Sexism and Culture: Japan's Obsession With Kawaii by AI Faithy Perez, In Savvy Tokyo: https://savvytokyo.com/sexism-culture-japans-obsession-kawaii/

Is there a Dark Side to The Those Adorable Bento Boxes? By Elizabeth Unger, In National Geographic: https://www.nationalgeographic.com/people-and-culture/food/the-plate/2016/01/28/is-there-a-dark-side-to-those-adorable-bento-boxes/

Sweet puppies and cute babies: perceptual adaptation to babyfacedness transfers across species by Fred Mast, in Academia: https://www.academia.edu/5943644/Sweet_puppies_and_cute_babies_perceptual_adaptation_to_babyfacedness_transfers_across_species?email_work_card=title

REFERENCES

Alario, S (2019), *Can You Dream It? Yes, I can.*, in Kristen Loreallo, accessed 22 September 2019 from <http://www.kristenlorello.com/can-you-dream-it-curated-by-scott-alario>

Amurgurumi Today (2019), *What is Amagurumi? Definition, History and Technique*, in Amurgurumi Today, accessed 25 September 2019 from <https://amigurumi.today/what-is-amigurumi/>

Artnet (2019), Yoshitomo Nara, in Artnet accessed 21 September 2019 from <http://www.artnet.com/artists/yoshitomo-nara/>

Austin, K (n.d.), *Elderspeak: Babytalk Directed at Older Adults*, in ChangingAging accessed 27 September 2019 from <https://changingaging.org/elderhood/elderspeak-babytalk-directed-at-older-adults/>

Baum-Haines, S (2016), *The Dark Side of These Cute Animals Will Make You Rethink Cuddly Creatures*, In Science 101, accessed September 2019 from <https://www.science101.com/dark-side-cute-animals-rethink-cuddly-creatures/>

Benson, L (2019), *Can You Dream It? Cuteness and Creativity*, In Elephant, accessed 22 September 2019 from <https://elephant.art/can-you-dream-it/>

Billseigs (2019), *Why doesn't that cat have a mouth? – Hello Kitty, the kawaii and children's culture of Japan*, In Kawaii Sekai, accessed 4 September 2019 from <http://kawaiisekai.com/hello-kitty/]>

Buckley, R (2016), *Aww: The Emotion of Perceiving Cuteness,* In Frontiers In Psychology, accessed 21 September 2019 from <https://www.frontiersin.org/articles/10.3389/fpsyg.2016.01740/full>

Burnett, D (2013), *Ugly animals rule, cute is creepy*, in The Guardian, accessed 26 September 2019, from <https://www.theguardian.com/science/brain-flapping/2013/sep/13/ugly-animals-preservation-cute-creepy>

Caudwell, C & Lacey, C (2017), *Super cute home robots are coming, but think twice before you trust them*, In The Conversation, accessed 22 September 2019 from <https://theconversation.com/super-cute-home-robots-are-coming-but-think-twice-before-you-trust-them-84428>

Caudwell, C & Lacey, C (2019), *What do home robots want? The ambivalent power of cuteness in robotic relationships*, In SAGE Journals, accessed 21 September 2019 from <https://journals.sagepub.com/doi/abs/10.1177/13548 56519837792?journalCode=cona>

CCFC: Campaign for a Commercial-Free Childhood (n.d.), *Hell No Barbie: 8 reasons to leave Hello Barbie on the shelf*, In CCFC, accessed September 2019 from <https://commercialfreechildhood.org/action/hell-no-barbie-8-reasons-leave-hello-barbie-shelf>

Crockett, Z (2018), *The Beanie Baby Bubble of '99*, In The Hustle, accessed 14 September 2019 from <https://thehustle.co/the-great-beanie-baby-bubble-of-99/>

Dale, JP (2017), Food & Drink: *The ultimate act of love? The truth behind Japan's charaben culture*, in CNN Travel: Food & Drink, accessed 24 September 2019 from

<https://edition.cnn.com/travel/article/japan-food-snap-power-of-cute-oped/index.html>

Getlen, L (2015), *How the Beanie Baby craze was concocted — then crashed*, In New York Post, accessed 15 September 2019 from <https://nypost.com/2015/02/22/how-the-beanie-baby-craze-was-concocted-then-crashed/>

Horton, R (2017), *Stop Infantilizing Old People, Please*, in HuffPost accessed September 2019 from <https://www.huffpost.com/entry/stop-infantilizing-old-people-please_b_8969134>

Kane, C (2016) *What Selfies in America vs. China Can Tell Us About Beauty Standards*, In Mic, accessed 18 September 2019 from <https://www.mic.com/articles/133484/what-selfies-in-america-vs-china-can-tell-us-about-beauty-standards>

Katz, B (2018), *Why We Want to Squeeze Cute, Little Things*, In Smithsonian, accessed 8 September 2019, from <https://www.smithsonianmag.com/smart-news/why-we-want-squeeze-cute-little-things-180971143/>

Keating, C. F. & Randall, DW & Kendrick, T & Gutshall, K. A. (2003), *Do babyfaced adults receive more help? The (cross-cultural) case of the lost resume*, Journal of Nonverbal Behavior, 27(2), 89e109, in ResearchGate, accessed 21 September 2019 from <https://www.researchgate.net/publication/22534652 0_The_Lost_E-Mail_Method_Milgram's_Lost-Letter_Technique_in_the_Age_of_the_Internet>

Kramer, L (2019), *41 cute logos that are totally aww-some*, In 99designs, accessed 9 September 2019 from <https://99designs.com/blog/creative-inspiration/cute-logos/>

Lobmaier, J. S., Sprengelmeyer, R., Wiffen, B., & Perrett, D. I. (2010). *Female and male responses to cuteness, age and emotion in infant faces.* Evolution and Human Behavior, 31(1), 16-21, In Science Direct, accessed 21 September 2019 from <https://www.sciencedirect.com/science/article/abs/pi i/S1090513809000531?via%3Dihub>

Madormo, C (n.d.), *The Untold Truth about Barbie*, in The List, accessed September 2019 from <https://www.thelist.com/90128/untold-truth-barbie/>

Marrs, M (2019), *What Are Teacup Dogs?*, In K9 of Mine accessed 28 September 2018 from <https://www.k9ofmine.com/teacup-pups/>

Martinez-Conde, S (2018), *6 Reasons Why We Love Small, Cute Things, According to Science*, In Mental Floss, accessed September 2019 from <http://mentalfloss.com/article/554311/reasons-why-we-love-small-cute-things-according-science>

Molloy, A (2014), *Concept of cuteness is 'hardwired from age of three,' say scientists*, In The Independent, accessed 24 September 2019 from <https://www.independent.co.uk/news/science/concept-of-cuteness-is-hardwired-from-age-of-three-say-scientists-9617791.html>

Molloy, M & Midgley, R (2017), *The dark side of the designer dog trend: Why it's cruel not cute*, In The Telegraph, accessed 28 September 2019 from <https://www.telegraph.co.uk/news/2017/09/14/dark-side-designer-dog-trend-cruel-not-cute/>

Morber, J (2018), *Why Cute Things Make Me Sad*, In The Globe and Mail, accessed 12 September 2019 from <https://www.theglobeandmail.com/opinion/article-why-cute-things-make-me-sad/>

Noone, Y (2016), *'Aww': Should this sound become the new human emotion to describe cuteness?*, In SBS: Special Broadcasting Service, accessed 19 September 2019 from <https://www.sbs.com.au/topics/life/health/article/2016/11/29/aww-should-sound-become-new-human-emotion-describe-cuteness>

O'Donnell, E (2019), *The Teddy Bear Effect*, from Harvard Magazine, in Harvard Kennedy School, accessed 22 September 2019 from <https://cpl.hks.harvard.edu/news/teddy-bear-effect>

Poltrack, E (2014), Why Do We Want to Bite Cute Things, Like Adorable Newborn Babies?, In Scientific American, accessed 10 September 2019 from <https://www.scientificamerican.com/article/why-do-we-want-to-bite-cute-things-like-adorable-newborn-babies/>

Robinson, KM (2017), *How Pets Help Manage Depression*, In WebMD, accessed 11 September 2019 from <https://www.webmd.com/depression/features/pets-depression#1>

Sebesfi, B (2019), *Cuteness vs Curiosity*, in Community Early Learning Australia (CELA), accessed 22 September 2019 from <https://www.cela.org.au/2019/07/01/cuteness/>

Shaw, J (2019), *What the 'meat paradox' reveals about moral decision making*, In BBC Future, accessed 21 September 2019 from <http://www.bbc.com/future/story/20190206-what-the-meat-paradox-reveals-about-moral-decision-making>

Shin, H (2016), *Be My Mother: Playful Home Appliance Robots*, In Hyerim Shin, accessed 22 September 2019 from <https://hyerimshin.com/be-my-mother>

Smith, RA (2019), *Those Cute Animal Videos on Twitter Have a Dark Side*, In Association of American Universities, accessed 27 September 2049 from <https://www.aau.edu/research-scholarship/featured-research-topics/those-cute-animal-videos-twitter-have-dark-side?

Steinman, R (2014), *Behavioral Bias Bingo — The Whimsical Cuteness Effect*, In Alpha Architect,

accessed 9 October 2019 from
<https://alphaarchitect.com/2014/10/07/behavioral-bias-bingo-the-whimsical-cuteness-effect/>

Suddath, C (2008), *A Brief History Of Mickey Mouse*, in TIME, accessed 3 September 2019 from
<http://content.time.com/time/arts/article/0,8599,1859935,00.html>

Vinopal, L (2018), *What Age Children are the Cutest, According to Science*, In Fatherly, accessed 24 September 2019 from
<https://www.fatherly.com/health-science/cutest-age-children-science/>

Volk, T., Franklin, P. & Wong, I. (2018), *Are newborns' faces less ap*pealing? Evolution and Human Behavior, Volume 39, Issue 3, May 2018, Pages 269-276, In Science Direct, accessed 24 September 2019 from
<https://www.sciencedirect.com/science/article/abs/pii/S1090513817303434?via%3Dihub>

Wallen, J (2016), *The not-so-cute side of emojis: Potential security, privacy, and bandwidth issues*, in TechRepublic, accessed 8 September 2019 from
<https://www.techrepublic.com/article/the-not-so-

cute-side-of-emojis-potential-security-privacy-and-bandwidth-issues/#targetText=The%20idea%20for%20emojis%20was,and%20forth%20with%20tiny%20images.>

Wang, S (n.d.) Animals Help People With Autism, PTSD, And Other Conditions, in SADAG: South African Depression and Anxiety Group, accessed 13 September 2019 from <

http://www.sadag.org/index.php?option=com_content&view=article&id=1958:animals-help-people-with-autism-ptsd-and-other-conditions&catid=37&Itemid=132>

Wapner, J (2017), *Marriage Therapy: Cute Animal Pictures Rekindle The Love, Study Finds*, in Newsweek: Tech & Science, accessed September 2018 from <https://www.newsweek.com/marriage-therapy-cute-animal-pictures-rekindle-love-study-finds-628644>

Wikipedia: The Free Encyclopedia (2019), *Hello Kitty*, In Wikipedia, accessed 2 September 2019 from <https://en.wikipedia.org/wiki/Hello_Kitty>

Wikipedia: The Free Encyclopedia (2019), *Japanese street fashion*, In Wikipedia, accessed September 2019 from

<https://en.wikipedia.org/wiki/Japanese_street_fashion#Decora

Zachos, E (2018), *This Is the Age When Puppies Are the Cutest, According to Science*, In National Geographic, accessed 26 September 2019 from <https://www.nationalgeographic.com/news/2018/05/puppies-dogs-cute-evolution-animals-spd/>

Zickfield, E; Kunst, JR; Hohle, SM (2017), *Too sweet to eat: Exploring the effects of cuteness on meat consumption*, 120th ed. [PDF.] Norway: Elsevier, pp.181-183, 191, In Academia.edu, accessed 21 September 2019 from <https://www.academia.edu/34629863/Too_sweet_to_eat_Exploring_the_effects_of_cuteness_on_meat_consumption>

READ OTHER

50 THINGS TO KNOW

BOOKS

50 Things to Know

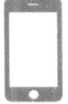

Stay up to date with new releases on Amazon:
https://amzn.to/2VPNGr7

Mailing List: Join the 50 Things to Know
Mailing List to Learn About New Releases

50 Things to Know

Please leave your honest review of this book on Amazon and Goodreads. We appreciate your positive and constructive feedback. Thank you.